A WOMAN of REST

6 studies for individuals
or groups

Phyllis J. Le Peau

Introductions by Linda Shands

With Guidelines for Leaders
and Study Notes

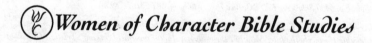
Women of Character Bible Studies

InterVarsity Press
Downers Grove, Illinois
Leicester, England

InterVarsity Press
P. O. Box 1400, Downers Grove, IL 60515, USA
38 De Montfort Street, Leicester LE1 7GP, England

©1997 by Phyllis J. Le Peau

Introductions ©1997 by Linda I. Shands

InterVarsity Press® is the book-publishing division of InterVarsity Christian Fellowship®, a student movement active on campus at hundreds of universities, colleges and schools of nursing in the United States of America, and a member movement of the International Fellowship of Evangelical Students. For information about local and regional activities, write Public Relations Dept., InterVarsity Christian Fellowship, 6400 Schroeder Rd., P.O. Box 7895, Madison, WI 53707-7895.

Inter-Varsity Press, UK, is the book-publishing division of the Universities and Colleges Christian Fellowship (formerly the Inter-Varsity Fellowship), a student movement linking Christian Unions in universities and colleges throughout the United Kingdom and the Republic of Ireland, and a member movement of the International Fellowship of Evangelical Students. For information about local and national activities write to UCCF, 38 De Montfort Street, Leicester LE1 7GP.

USA ISBN 0-8308-2048-5
UK ISBN 0-85111-389-3

Printed in the United States of America ♾

19	18	17	16	15	14	13	12	11	10	9	8	7	6	5	4	3	2	1
13	12	11	10	09	08	07	06	05	04	03	02	01	00	99	98	97		

Contents

Introducing *A Woman of Rest*   5

1. Jesus' Invitation to Rest
   Matthew 11:28-30   10

2. God's Gift of Food and Rest
   Exodus 16:1-30   16

3. Resting in God's Power
   Psalm 127   23

4. Resting in God's Presence
   Exodus 33:1-17   30

5. Resting in Belief in God
   Hebrews 3:1—4:11   36

6. Resting in God's Purpose
   Luke 2:21-40   43

Guidelines for Leaders   49

Study Notes   53

Cast of Characters

Setting the Stage

Each study's introduction takes the perspective of a different character in a continuing story to introduce the theme of each study. Below are the voices behind each introduction.

1 *Barbara* —the bride's mother

2 *Hope* —the bride's older sister

3 *Barbara*

4 *Angela* —the bride

5 *Barbara*

6 *Melissa* — Hope's daughter, the bridesmaid

Other Characters

Doug —the bridegroom

The Augsbergs — Doug's parents

Grandma/Gran —the bride's grandmother

The church secretary

Introducing *A Woman of Rest*

We are cursed with a frenetic compulsion. When we get in the car, we fill the silence by turning on the radio. When we get home, we fill the room with company by turning on the TV. If the weekend is unscheduled, we cook up some activity to keep us occupied—an odd job, an errand or a night at the theater. Even our vacations are so filled with driving, sightseeing, sports activities and visiting relatives that we return home exhausted, in need of a break.

We are afraid to stop because we might discover that we are rushing as fast as we can *without a destination*. Without some activity to give ourselves identity or our lives meaning, we might have to face ourselves and despair at the emptiness we see. So it is do, do, do in a joyless rush to block out our fears.

Our busyness is sin. In our rushing we reject God. His fourth commandment to us was one of rest.

We are to bring our lives periodically to a halt for two reasons. First, it is good for us. Our mental, emotional, spiritual and physical condition are in better health and balance when we rest. Our joys are deeper and our troubles can be handled with more ease. Rest itself is a pleasure to be savored and enjoyed on its own. Second, rest is a statement of our faith and trust in God that he will watch over and care for us even when we do nothing to help ourselves. Not to rest is to commit the sin of unbelief.

Both men and women in society face this problem, though sometimes in different ways. Men are often driven to busyness in their jobs or other tasks as a prime source of self-identity. Women often busy themselves in caring, nurturing roles (whether on the job, at church, in the home or in the community) to fill their needs for self-esteem.

The introductions in this guide are parts of a continuing story. In this story we meet women who struggle to maintain God's perspective in the midst of wedding preparations. They succeed in some areas and fail in others. However, their love and caring for each other even in the hard times and misunderstandings comes through.

This study guide will examine these issues of busyness and rest for women in the light of key passages of Scripture which direct our hearts and minds back to God and his priorities for our lives.

Suggestions for Individual Study

1. As you begin each study pray that God will speak to you through his Word.

2. Read the introduction to the study, "Setting the Stage," and respond to the questions that follow it. The story is designed to draw you into the topic at hand and help you begin to see how the Scripture relates to daily life. If there will be a week or more between your studies, then you may want to read all of the introductions in one sitting to get the flow of the ongoing story. This will help if you find that you are having trouble keeping track of all the characters.

3. This is an inductive Bible study, designed to help you discover for yourself what Scripture is saying. Each study deals with a particular passage—so that you can really delve into the author's meaning in that context. Read and reread the passage to be studied. The questions are written using the language of the New International Version, so you may wish to use that version of the Bible. The New Revised Standard Version is also recommended.

4. "God's Word for Us" includes three types of questions. *Observation* questions ask about the basic facts: who, what, when, where and how. *Interpretation* questions delve into the meaning of the passage. *Application* questions (also found in the "Now or Later" section) help you discover the implications of the text for growing in Christ. These three keys unlock the treasures of Scripture.

Write your answers to the study questions in the spaces provided or in a personal journal. Writing can bring clarity and deeper understanding of yourself and of God's Word.

5. Use the study notes at the back of the guide to gain additional insight and information after you have worked through the questions for yourself.

6. Move to the "Now or Later" section. These are ideas for you to freely use in closing your study and responding to God. You may want to choose one of these to do right away and continue working through the other ideas on subsequent days to reinforce what you are learning.

Suggestions for Members of a Group Study

1. Come to the study prepared. Follow the suggestions for individual study mentioned above. You will find that careful preparation will greatly enrich your time spent in group discussion.

2. Be willing to participate in the discussion. The leader of your group will not be lecturing. Instead, she will be encouraging the members of the group to discuss what they have learned. The leader will be asking the questions that are found in this guide.

3. Stick to the topic being discussed. Your answers should be based on the verses which are the focus of the discussion and not on outside authorities such as commentaries or speakers. These studies focus on a particular passage of Scripture. Only rarely should you refer to other portions of the Bible. This allows for everyone to participate on equal ground and for in-depth study.

4. Be sensitive to the other members of the group. Listen attentively when they describe what they have learned. You may be surprised by their insights! Each question assumes a variety of answers. Many questions do not have "right" answers, particularly questions that aim at meaning or application. Instead the questions push us to explore the passage more thoroughly.

When possible, link what you say to the comments of others. Also, be affirming whenever you can. This will encourage some of the more hesitant members of the group to participate.

5. Be careful not to dominate the discussion. We are sometimes so eager to express our thoughts that we leave too little opportunity for others to respond. By all means participate! But allow others to also.

6. Expect God to teach you through the passage being

discussed and through the other members of the group. Pray that you will have an enjoyable and profitable time together, but also that as a result of the study, you will find ways that you can take action individually and/or as a group.

7. It will be helpful for groups to follow a few basic guidelines. These guidelines, which you may wish to adapt to your situation, should be read at the beginning of the first session.

☐ Anything said in the group is considered confidential and will not be discussed outside the group unless specific permission is given to do so.

☐ We will provide time for each person present to talk if he or she feels comfortable doing so.

☐ We will talk about ourselves and our own situations, avoiding conversation about other people.

☐ We will listen attentively to each other.

☐ We will be very cautious about giving advice.

☐ We will pray for each other.

8. If you are the group leader, you will find additional suggestions at the back of the guide.

1

Jesus' Invitation to Rest

Matthew 11:28-30

 SETTING THE STAGE:

Barbara, Mother of the Bride

You can stare at Angie's wedding portrait until you're blue in the face and still not see the strain. Nonetheless it's there; in the weary-grey shadows beneath her eyes, and the minuscule wrinkles on her forehead—hair-thin cracks on the face of a porcelain doll.

Just before I snapped the picture, a breeze ruffled her veil and she raised one hand to smooth it back. Her cheeks look flushed; her smile bright enough to light up midnight.

I place the picture in its pewter frame back on the mantle and turn away. I can almost feel her eyes follow me across the room.

"Meddler!" If she could shout it, I wouldn't dispute her.

I swing around, but her face remains in profile, chin tilted upward, intent on the look of adoration in her bridegroom's eyes.

I should have kept quiet. When she came home that night, waggling her ring finger and babbling with excitement, I should have laughed with her, or maybe even cried, and said, "That's wonderful, darling, when's the happy day?"

I was delighted of course. She and Douglas Augsburg were the perfect match.

Then she informed me, "The wedding is in June."

I distinctly remember the feeling of irritation that caused me to raise my voice. "June! Do you realize that's only four months away?"

How would I ever manage? I still had a thousand phone calls to make for the Charity Bazaar, and I was the main speaker for the Woman's Guild banquet at the end of May.

I should have backed off then, hugged her and inquired about her plans. Instead I bristled like a startled cat. "That won't do, Angela. I can't possibly pull anything together until at least September."

She was the one who stayed calm. "Doug leaves for Europe in July, remember? I'm going with him. It's all arranged." She closed her eyes and smiled, caught up in her dreams. "Don't worry, Mother, we've decided on a small wedding. Just family and a few close friends."

I pulled myself together. "Now, we'll have no nonsense about a small wedding. The Augsburgs never do anything on a small scale. There will be at least a hundred guests from their side alone."

I saw the panic in her eyes. Then her face went blank, hands frozen into fists at her sides. I realize now she took that stance whenever we had a disagreement and she knew she couldn't win. I had never let it stop me before, and I didn't let it stop me then.

"We'll have Chantel's arrange the flowers," I said, measuring her waistline with my eyes. "Your grandmother's gown is still in the cedar chest . . ." Then it hit me. "Oh, good grief, what about the church? It will be impossible to book a June wedding at this late date."

I rushed straight to the telephone. Angela yelled something about it being her wedding, and shouldn't she have a say? But before we could decide a thing, I had to talk to the church secretary.

By the time we had the date and time worked out, Angela had run upstairs. What I really wanted was a long hot bath, but there was so much to think about. The flowers, candles, music. The bridesmaid's dress.

It did cross my mind that maybe I should wait and pray. If I had, perhaps things would not have happened as they did. As it was, I ignored the impulse to stop and bow my head. After all, we had to get the invitations out.

"This is impossible," I remember saying to myself as I searched the desktop for my address book. But in my mind I was convinced I could manage it.

---

1. How does Barbara's attitude in the last couple paragraphs characterize how most Christians look at their lives?

---

2. Your need for rest may not come from a major event like a wedding, but from the daily routine. What factors in your life are currently wearing you down?

GOD'S WORD FOR US
Read Matthew 11:28-30.

3. In your own words describe Jesus' invitation.

4. What conditions are necessary for receiving Jesus' rest?

5. What causes you to feel wearied and burdened?

6. What do you think it means "to find rest" in the fullest sense?

7. What keeps you from coming to Jesus with your burdens?

8. What about Jesus is attractive to you as you think about learning about rest from him?

---

9. What is the result of working in the yoke with Jesus?

Why do you think this happens?

---

10. What do you think you have to learn from Jesus that would produce a restful lifestyle for you?

---

11. How would being yoked to Jesus help you produce rest for others?

 NOW OR LATER

Ideas to close your group meeting or personal study or for continued daily reflection.

☐ Read Psalm 23. Spend time reflecting on it.

   See: Sunny, green pastures where wild flowers are abundant.

Feel: A gentle breeze and the warmth of the sun.

Hear: A babbling brook, gently overflowing the pond.

Imagine: You are a sheep grazing with other sheep. Jesus, the shepherd, stands watchful, holding his staff. Nothing threatens you because you are near him. The shepherd has provided this safe place for you. Relax. Enjoy being with him. Rest in the grass.

☐ Journal on the following questions:

How would you respond if a friend offered to take all of your burdens and carry them for you?

What do you need to more fully experience the rest that Jesus offers you today?

How would you explain to a person seeking to know God how to experience Jesus' rest?

☐ Write a prayer to Jesus about what you need to respond to his invitation to rest.

2

....

God's Gift of
Food and Rest

Exodus 16:1-30

 SETTING THE STAGE:

Hope, Sister of the Bride

I carefully smooth the wafer-thin silk and tuck filmy plastic around folds of antique ivory lace. Hanging the fragile bundle in the entry hall, I make a mental note to drop it off at the cleaners tomorrow. Having my sister's gown preserved is my final contribution to her wedding.

I remember when Mother called to tell me Angie was getting married. "Will you do the cake?" she asked. "Oh, and those little petit fours. The one's with the colored icing?"

Of course, I said, "Yes." Then on impulse I added, "Tell Angie I'll help with the dresses too."

Mother hesitated; a whisper of relief shading her concern. "Are you sure, Hope? You work full time as it is."

I thought about my job at the bakery where I worked forty hours a week. How else could we afford to pay for this house? Not to mention braces, piano lessons and summer camp.

"There's always evenings and weekends," I said

brightly. "Who needs to eat or sleep?"

That was supposed to be a joke.

I push the memory aside and slip more flimsy plastic over my daughter's bridesmaid's dress; a figure-hugging, lavender brocade.

When we went to pick out material, I almost overrode their decision on the pattern. High necked. Bare shouldered. Ankle length with a slit from hem to knee. Much too sophisticated for a thirteen-year-old, but Melissa was so excited, and this was Angie's choice; I couldn't turn them down.

Hooking the hanger over the rod in Melissa's closet, I'm reminded it took six hours of overtime to pay for the material. Sophisticated or not, I'll have to let her wear it again.

Mother had always planned for Angie to have Grandma's wedding gown, but the material had yellowed with age, and no cleaner in town would touch it. "It can't be restored." Mother was in tears, but Angie looked relieved.

"We've got four months," I reminded them and took Angie back to the fabric store.

I decorated cakes at the bakery all day, and we worked on Angie's gown at night. For weeks, I handstitched lace covered buttons in my sleep. Melissa got her own meals, but it was easier for me to grab a cup of coffee and a pastry at work. I skipped church on Sundays and told myself that serving my family was the same as serving the Lord.

Looking back, I'm not sure when the dizzy spells started. "Just tired," I thought as my knees went suddenly weak, or a tube of icing fell out of my shaking hands.

"You've probably got the flu," Mother sympathized. "You had better take some time off work, Hope. We can't have you sick for your sister's wedding. Remember, we're counting on you."

"You and a million other people." I muttered and headed for the bakery to ice and freeze another batch of petit fours.

Melissa's dress was all cut out; paper pinned fabric draped over the back of a dining room chair.

"Why can't I, like, help?" she must have asked a hundred times.

"Because," I'd snap, "I don't have time to show you." Then I'd apologize for my tone of voice and promise her we'd get to it soon. And we would have, but two weeks before the wedding everything came to a screeching halt.

Mother blames herself, but of course it wasn't her fault. None of us can control the circumstances life hands out.

1. In what ways do you identify with Hope's desire to serve her family?

What are the potential dangers of telling yourself that serving your family is the same as serving the Lord?

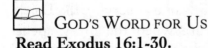 GOD'S WORD FOR US
Read Exodus 16:1-30.

2. This took place three days after the Lord miraculously led the Israelites out of Egypt. The Israelites had safely walked through the Red Sea onto dry land. Pharaoh's horses, chariots and horsemen were destroyed by this same Red Sea because the Lord brought its waters back over them. Exodus 15:1-21 is a description of this incident and is filled with songs of praise to God for his great faithfulness to them. What is the attitude of the Israelites in Exodus 16:1-30?

_____

3. How does God respond to the Israelites each time they ask for or look for food (vv. 4, 11-12, 28-29)?

_____

4. How are you like the Israelites and how are you different from them in the way that they grumbled against the Lord?

_____

5. When have you thought you were grumbling against others, but it was really the Lord who was the target of your complaints?

_____

6. What were the Lord's instructions concerning gathering meat and bread (vv. 4-5)? (What were his specific instructions about the Sabbath?)

7. What happened when these instructions were followed and when they were not followed (vv. 15-30)?

8. Read Exodus 20:8-11. What must we believe about God in order to follow his instructions about regular rest?

9. Often in our lives God's instructions about work and resting from work are not followed. What causes you to be driven in your work and life?

10. Time and again, the Lord said, "Then you will know that I am the Lord your God." How is your relationship with God affected when you are consumed by your work and acquiring things and do not follow God's instructions concerning rest from work?

11. How is a life of dependence on and trust in God to meet all our needs a prerequisite to experiencing Sabbath rest?

12. What are barriers you need to overcome and changes you need to make in order to have periods of rest in your life?

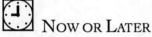 NOW OR LATER
☐ Read Genesis 1:1—2:3. Reflect on God's work. How did God do his work? How does he feel about his work? Write down your impressions.

Notice the repeated phrase "and the evening and the morning were the first day." God is already working as we sleep. How does that thought contrast to our usual thinking that everything starts in the morning when we first get up?

What do you feel as you read the description of the seventh day? Write down your thoughts about what it is or could be like for you to rest regularly.

☐ Write a prayer to God the Creator. Praise him for his wonderful works, for the joy he has in his creation and the great value that he places on it. Thank him for his invitation to and provision for rest. Ask him to reveal attitudes of pride and grumbling in you. Confess your sins of refusing to rest and to take time away from your work as he has instructed us to do.

3

Resting in God's Power

Psalm 127

 SETTING THE STAGE:

Barbara, Mother of the Bride

I study my own face in the gilt frame mirror hanging on the dining room wall. A gift from the Augsbergs, "For hosting the wedding, my dear. No one else could have pulled it off."

The lines around my own eyes, carved by something deeper than age, have yet to disappear. I would have thought a few full nights of sleep would have at least caused them to fade.

It's not like I've never planned a wedding. A thousand little details, yes, but they should have all fallen into place, each step following the other, like pages on a calandar. Organization—that's what gets the job done.

How could I have missed the most important part?

"You mean this June?" the secretary at Westside Baptist sounded as incredulous as I'd felt when Angela insisted on that date.

"I'm sorry, dear, there's graduation, you know, a fiftieth anniversary and three other weddings. I'm afraid there's not a weekend to be had."

Hope told me once, "Mother, if persistence was a virtue, you'd be a candidate for sainthood!" She was being facetious, of course, but I'm afraid she was right.

"We're founding members of that church," I reminded the woman. "Surely you can do something."

"Oh, well then," she finally gave in, "what about a Monday night?"

Not ideal, but it would have to do.

Then there were the little disappointments. I pictured candles at the end of every pew. But the fire marshall would not allow it. Angela asked for a popular music piece and you'd have thought we wanted to hire a hard rock band.

Ms. Augsburg must have changed her guest list fifty times and then insisted on champagne and dancing at the reception, which meant we couldn't hold it at the church.

Angela grew more distant with every change of plans, and none of us was sleeping well. I'd creep up the stairs at two a.m. and find light seeping from the crack beneath her bedroom door.

She and Hope assured me they were almost finished with her dress. "I'll give a nice luncheon," I told them, "just the women in the family. We'll discuss the final details, then Angela and Melissa will put on a fashion show."

All those carefully laid plans.

The day Hope fainted, I rushed to the hospital, my heart racing like a caged wild bird. She lay so white and still, fragile as an eggshell, stretched out on hospital sheets. A fire-red gash closed with ugly black stitches tracked across her brow. I stepped aside as a nurse wrapped half a roll of gauze around the wound.

Hope had cut her foot on broken glass when she was six, and sprained her wrist playing volleyball in junior high, but she had never been unconscious before. Thirty-one hours. It seemed like a lifetime.

The doctors were optimistic. The diagnosis—hypertension caused by stress. "She has a concussion," they said. "And we have to get her blood pressure down. When she wakes up, she'll need medication and several weeks of bed rest."

Two weeks from Monday was Angela's wedding day.

We took turns at Hope's bedside, holding her hand and praying. Wedding plans were pushed aside until her eyes finally fluttered open and she said, "Mother, I'm not feeling well, you'll have to finish Melissa's dress."

I laughed until I cried.

---

1. In what ways do you identify with Barbara's growing feelings of pressure and anxiety?

 GOD'S WORD FOR US
Read Psalm 127.

2. What warning is given about labor?

3. In your own words describe the anxiety spoken of in verse 2.

4. How is this kind of anxiety a description of your work and life?

5. Do you think that this psalm is suggesting that God is doing everything so we should sit back and do nothing? Explain.

6. How does taking God seriously help us to reach the balance between frantic activity and passivity?

7. The psalmist seems to abruptly move from the topic of labor to the topic of children. What does he say about children?

8. How is building a house (v. 1) like building a family (vv. 3-5)?

9. What have you learned from this study which will help you to rest in God's work?

10. According to verse 2, it is the Lord who gives those he loves sleep. What do you need in order to receive this gift of deep rest from him?

 NOW OR LATER

☐ Read John 17:1-5. This is Jesus' prayer at the end of his earthly life as he faces the cross. What seems to be the condition of his spirit?

What are Jesus' requests in this first paragraph?

What is life?

How has Jesus brought glory to the Father?

How do you respond to the confident statement of Jesus, "I have finished the work that you gave me to do"?

☐ Reflect on the following statements and journal on your impressions.

Hilary of Tours diagnosed our desperate busyness as, "a blasphemous anxiety to do God's work for him."

"We are going about trying desperately for our presence to make a difference." — Henri Nouwen

"Our work should be just as enjoyable as having children." — Eugene Peterson

"The first great fact which emerges from our civilization is that today everything has become 'means.' There is no longer an 'end'; we do not know whither we are going. We have forgotten our collective ends, and we possess great means: we get huge machines in motion in order to arrive nowhere." — Jacques Ellul

☐ Write a prayer to Jesus acknowledging your need for him to build the house and guard the city. Talk about your tendency to attempt to work alone, apart from him. Thank him for the sleep that he gives—pure and deep sleep.

4

....

Resting in God's Presence

Exodus 33:1-17

 SETTING THE STAGE:

Angela, the Bride

I like quiet times and simple things. I like strolling on the beach at sunrise, feeding pigeons in the square and exactly what I'm doing now—sipping iced coffee at a sidewalk cafe while I wait for Doug to come and walk me back to our hotel. At least this time I'm not afraid.

I spent too many nights waiting when the fear was real. I'd pray awhile, then watch the moon cast tree-branch shadows across Mother's manicured lawn. I'd close my eyes and dream that Doug was waiting too, in the darkness underneath my window, to sweep me up and carry me away.

Fairytale stuff. But we'd talked about it so often. When he was at the base, he called every night before he went on duty. "Why can't we just elope?" I'd moan, especially after a day when Mother had been difficult, or there'd been another change in *her* wedding plans.

"I guess we should have," Doug would agree, "but it's too late now. Both of our mothers would have our heads."

Then his voice would grow soft and soothing. "Just a little longer, Angie. Wait for me? I'll make it up to you, I promise."

We'd murmur goodnight, blow kisses into the phone, and I'd ask the Lord to help me make it through another lonely night.

I don't have Hope's patience, or Mother's tenacity. I wanted a simple wedding, something that could be accomplished without a lot of fuss. As usual, Mother had other ideas. I resented her interfering, but I knew from experience it was easier to just give in. I told Doug, "At least with Mom in charge, every detail will be perfect."

It's not that she didn't try. If things hadn't happened the way they did, my wedding would have been the social event of the century.

I remember Gran saying, "Sometimes our striving is like screaming against the wind; when it gets too rough, it's best to just be quiet and listen." Some of us should have taken her advice!

I guess I'll never understand why God allows some things to happen. When Hope passed out, I felt awful. She'd been working too hard, doing extra things for Mom and me. It did make me realize how much my big sister loved me.

The Sunday we brought her home from the hospital, Doug called at the usual time, so when I heard his voice again at one o'clock on Monday afternoon, I knew something was wrong. "My squadron leaves tonight," he whispered. "They won't say for how long, and I can't tell you where we're going. I'm so sorry, Angie. I love you."

It sounded so final. Just remembering makes me cry.

"Why, God?" I must have asked a thousand times. "Why does he have to go now?" I tried not to think about where he was, or why, but I knew he was in danger and the waiting hurt worse than any other kind of pain.

I take a sip of frothy mocha, lift my face and let the warm wind dry my cheeks. Doug will be here soon and I don't want him to see me cry. So I relax and call up happy memories instead: Candles flickering on the mantle. Lavender rose buds on the cake. The baby's breath grandma tucked in my bouquet.

I think about the way I feel when he holds me: like being wrapped in an eiderdown quilt, or waking up to birdsong after a bad dream. Like leaping from the shadows into light.

---

1. How is Angela's life during her engagement different from what she expected?

---

2. When have you felt a strong need for God's presence with you?

 GOD'S WORD FOR US
Read Exodus 33:1-11.

---

3. In study two we looked at the Israelites at the beginning of their journey in the wildnerness. This passage looks at the other end of that journey. They are about to enter the Promised Land. Describe in your own words all that is happening between God and Moses and the Israelites (vv. 1-6).

4. What happened at the tent of meeting (vv. 7-11)?

5. What is significant about the fact that God provided a tent of meeting for his people?

6. Think about your relationship with God. In what ways do you identify with the Israelites?

Read Exodus 33:12-17.

7. Moses carries on a direct and honest conversation with God. What are Moses' concerns (vv. 12-17)?

8. How do your concerns in life compare and contrast with those of Moses?

9. How are you affected by the fact that God knows you by name (vv. 12, 17)?

---

10. God promised Moses that his presence would go with him and that he would give him rest as a result of this. What do you think this rest means?

---

11. In what ways does God's presence with you distinguish you and your Christian community (v. 16)?

---

12. As you reflect on this passage, what does it mean to you to rest in God's presence?

 NOW OR LATER

☐ Read Psalm 91. Reflect on this passage. What are the benefits of being so close to the Lord that you are under his shadow?

☐ Journal on the following: Describe what it is like to be

in the presence of one you dearly love and with whom you feel totally safe. How does this compare and/or contrast with how you feel about being in God's presence?

Jesus kept a demanding schedule but regularly took time to be with his Father. He recognized his dependence on his Father and his need for renewal. How would you compare and contrast your dependence on the Father and your need for renewal?

□ Write a prayer to the Father. Tell him of your need for him or your desire to know your need for him. Talk about difficulty that you have in getting time with him and what you need to do about it. Confess to him your lack of desire to rest in his presence. Ask him to renew your hunger for him and to help you to seek your rest in him.

5

Resting in Belief in God

Hebrews 3:1 — 4:11

 SETTING THE STAGE:

Barbara, Mother of the Bride

It amazes me how quickly we fall back into old habits. A few days later, I settled Hope between her own flowered sheets, stocked her freezer with casseroles and instructed Melissa how to heat them.

"Either Angela or I will check in every day," I promised Hope. "I'll sew Melissa's dress while the girls tie birdseed into those squares of lavender netting. You can help with that. I found some tiny white satin ribbon, and I thought we could tuck a sprig of baby's breath into each bow."

The phone call came the next afternoon. Angela took it in her room, but came downstairs only a few minutes later, her eyes wild, her face bloodless with shock. She looked at me and whispered, "Mamma . . . ?"

She hadn't called me Mamma since she was two.

I knew something was terribly wrong, but I didn't have the breath to ask. I just took her in my arms and held her, both of us trembling, until she quit sobbing long enough to say, "Doug's squad is leaving on a mission. He won't be back in time for the wedding."

His destination was secret, and most likely dangerous, or they would not have sent him off so fast. We had no way of knowing if or when he would come home. I knew Angela's every thought was sharpened by fear.

Those first few hours, I felt like a robot encased in human skin. I canceled the church and the flowers, wrapped candles in tissue paper and organized a telephone chain to inform 200 people, "The wedding has been postponed." I refused to allow anyone to use the word *canceled*.

I thawed a container of homemade soup and took half of it to Hope's. We shed fresh tears, then Melissa assured me, "Moms and I will be, like, fine."

I had to smile. Capable Melissa. I hadn't realized she was so grown up.

Back home, the mingled scents of chicken broth and sun-warmed roses accompanied me up the stairs to Angela's open bedroom door. My poor baby. She lay across her bed, wet lashes drooping over swollen, red-rimmed eyes. Her skin looked flushed, her cheeks felt warm against my cool palm. She didn't stir and I tiptoed away. Sleep, like laughter, brings healing.

Midnight. The ticking of my glass-domed anniversary clock reminded me that life goes on, even when it feels as if the world has toppled down around your ears.

I sat in the darkness for a while, praying for Douglas and both of my girls. When my mind wandered back to the chaos of the last few months, I couldn't help but moan, "All that wasted time!"

But was it wasted, really? Douglas would return eventually and the wedding could go on as planned. The church was out, of course. They'd been kind enough to say they'd hold that Monday night, but I knew in my bones it wouldn't be that soon.

There had to be another way, but I was too exhausted to figure it out.

I lifted my Bible from the bedside table. A thin black ribbon marked the place where I'd left off. I couldn't begin to remember how long ago.

The passage marked was John 14, with verse 27 underlined in red.

"Peace I leave with you; my peace I give you. . . . Do not let your hearts be troubled and do not be afraid."

Jesus was speaking, and I closed my tired eyes to listen.

---

1. As Barbara's story continues, at last we see her resting in Jesus' presence. What did it take to get her there?

What do you think this was like for her?

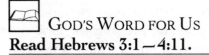

GOD'S WORD FOR US
Read Hebrews 3:1 — 4:11.

---

2. What kinds of rest are spoken of in this passage?

3. What similarities between the Israelites entering the Promised Land and Christians entering God's rest do you see throughout this passage?

4. According to 3:1-6, why were the Jewish Christians to fix their thoughts on Jesus?

5. List all that is said about Jesus in 3:1-6.

How do these facts encourage you to rest in him?

6. What do you think the writer meant when he spoke of being hardened by sin's deceitfulness (3:12-15)?

Why do you think encouraging one another prevents this hardening?

7. According to 4:1-3, like the Israelites, we have the gospel preached to us with the invitation to enter God's rest. What kind of rest is described in these verses?

_____

8. Why is it significant that "rest" is the name the writer gives to entering into a relationship with God?

_____

9. What strong warnings and admonitions are given in 4:1-7 concerning this relationship?

_____

10. Verse 9 says that there remains, that there is still left or left to come, a Sabbath-rest for the people of God. How does anticipation of that final day of rest affect you right now?

_____

11. What is the place of the Word of God in our lives as we seek to rest in belief?

12. It says in 4:10 "for anyone who enters God's rest also rests from his own work." In looking back over this whole passage which type of rest from God do you find to be a challenge for you?

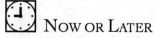 NOW OR LATER

☐ Read Mark 9:17-26. If you were this father what would you be feeling?

How does the father deal with his own unbelief?

How is this a model for you as you desire to rest in belief?

☐ Journal on the following: How is my freedom to rest affected by my believing or not believing God?

How is my freedom to rest affected by obeying or not obeying God?

"I long for the final comsummation of the Sabbath, when God's kingdom will reign supreme and alone. When the final day of this world comes, all our attempts to be God will be ended in the Joy of his triumphant presence."
—Marva Dawn

☐ Someone has said that "not believing God" is the basis of all sin. Reflect on the sin of disbelief. Ask God to reveal specific ways in which you sin against him by not believing him. Wait quietly before him and write down what the Holy Spirit brings to mind. Talk to God about each area. Confess your sin and receive his forgiveness.

6

Resting in God's Purpose

Luke 2:21-40

 SETTING THE STAGE:

Melissa, Bridesmaid

Who says a wedding has to be in church? If you ask me, I don't think God cares. Anyway, this whole wedding thing has been so weird. I told them Doug would come home sooner or later. So why the big time stress? It's not like he can help it or anything. The Air Force is his job.

Angie said she knew that. She knew she'd have to get used to it too, if she was going to marry him. But she cried all the time anyway, and I thought, "Geesh, maybe I'll just stay single."

With Mom sick, and Nana busy cancelling everything, I figured it was up to me to finish my dress. It was, like, no big deal. The machine was all set up, and I'd been sewing t-shirts and stuff since the seventh grade. I just said a prayer and followed the pattern.

Was I right? Doug called Angie on July first and I made her tell me word for word. "We just got in," he said. "I'll be home in two days. Do you still want to marry me?"

You'd think he'd been gone a year. Angie cried because

he was coming home, Moms cried because she was still suppose to stay in bed, and Nana flew into cyberspace. "Melissa, you'll just have to do the flowers. I've got two days and we are going to have this wedding!"

I said, "Cool!"

Angie helped. We picked some sprigs of lilac from the bush next to the porch, and Mom said to cut every rose that was anything close to a bud. We wrapped them in bunches with wet paper towels, then set them on newspaper in the back of Angie's car.

When we got to Nana's, the vases were scrubbed and ready. Nana sounded like a drill sergeant. "Angela, the bakery called. The cake is ready, and don't forget the petit fours. Melissa, you can help in the kitchen."

Boy, did the ladies from church come through with the goodies! Nuts and mints in silver dishes and little sandwiches shaped like hearts. I made cran-raspberry punch, and poured it in the good crystal punch bowl.

Some men set up the folding chairs. Then they rolled a bolt of white material down the stairs, across the carpet to the fireplace where Pastor and the rest of us would stand.

The living room smelled like a garden. Moms said, "I've rested enough," and set bouquets of lilacs and roses everywhere.

I got dressed in Angie's room and helped her fix her veil. Doug wasn't supposed to see her, but I went down and snapped his picture with my Instamatic. He gave me a hug and a kiss on the cheek. "Whoa," I thought, "I hope I find someone like him to marry."

Everything was cool until the photographer called. His car broke down or something. Anyway he couldn't make it till four and the ceremony was set for noon. I thought

Nana would loose it for sure, but she just bowed her head a minute then smiled and said, "Didn't I see Melissa with a camera?"

All the pictures turned out neat. Here's one of Aunt Angie and me standing by the fountain in Nana's back yard. Nana said, "Melissa, you look like a Sterling rosebud in that dress," and Moms said, "It's okay, Missy, she means well," and I said, "What a cool wedding. Hey, you guys, think about it. In a few years we'll be doing this for me!"

---

1. How did God teach Melissa about his purposes through Angie's wedding?

2. When has God revealed his purposes to you through a seemingly strange set of circumstances?

 GOD'S WORD FOR US
Read Luke 2:21-40.

---

3. Describe the setting of this story.

---

4. What do you learn about Simeon (vv. 22-25)?

about Anna (vv. 36-38)?

_____

5. What do you think is Simeon's view of and/or relationship with God?

What is Anna's?

_____

6. How did their perception of God and his purpose seem to affect their daily lives?

_____

7. To what degree do you think God has a purpose for you?

_____

8. What hope do Simeon and Anna offer the family?

9. How do Simeon and Anna also offer the family a mixed blessing?

10. How do you see a mixture of hope and barriers to hope in your own life?

11. How do Mary and Joseph move forward in the purpose God has for them (vv. 39-40)?

12. How have you been affected by others who have rested in God and his purpose for them?

13. What have you learned from Simeon and Anna that will help you to rest in God and his purposes?

NOW OR LATER

☐ Journal on the following: What is it like for me to have to wait for something important?

☐ Reflect on the following passages:

"He gives strength to the weary and increases the power of the weak. Even youths grow tired and weary, and young men stumble and fall; but those who hope in the LORD will renew their strength. They will soar on wings like eagles; they will run and not grow weary, they will walk and not be faint." (Isaiah 40:29-31)

"I will stand at my watch and station myself on the ramparts; I will look to see what he will say to me, and what answer I am to give to this complaint." (Habakkuk 2:1)

Wait before the Lord, quietly, to hear whatever he has to say to you. Write down what he says.

Guidelines for Leaders

My grace is sufficient for you. (2 Corinthians 12:9)

If leading a Bible study is something new for you, don't worry. These studies are designed to be led easily. As a matter of fact, the flow of questions through the passage from observation to interpretation to application is so natural that you may feel that the studies lead themselves.

You don't need to be an expert on the Bible or a trained teacher to lead a Bible discussion. The idea behind these inductive studies is that the leader guides group members to discover for themselves what the Bible has to say. This method of learning will allow group members to remember much more of what is said than a lecture would.

This study guide is flexible. You can use it with a variety of groups—student, professional, neighborhood or church groups. Each study takes about forty-five minutes in a group setting with the possibility of extending the time to sixty minutes or more by adding questions from "Now or Later."

There are some important facts to know about group dynamics and encouraging discussion. The suggestions listed below should enable you to effectively and enjoyably fulfill your role as leader.

Preparing for the Study

1. Ask God to help you understand and apply the passage in your own life. Unless this happens, you will not be prepared to lead others. Pray too for the various members of the group. Ask God to open your hearts to the message of his Word and motivate you to action.

2. Read the introduction to the entire guide to get an overview of the subject at hand and the issues which will be explored. Also read through the introductions to each study to get the flow of the

continuing story that runs through the guide and to get familiar with the characters. Be ready to refer the group to the list of characters on the back of the contents page if they have questions about the story.

3. As you begin each study, read and reread the assigned Bible passage to familiarize yourself with it.

4. This study guide is based on the New International Version of the Bible. It will help you and the group if you use this translation as the basis for your study and discussion.

5. Carefully work through each question in the study. Spend time in meditation and reflection as you consider how to respond.

6. Write your thoughts and responses in the space provided in the study guide. This will help you to express your understanding of the passage clearly.

7. It might help you to have a Bible dictionary handy. Use it to look up any unfamiliar words, names or places. (For additional help on how to study a passage, see chapter five of *Leading Bible Discussions*, InterVarsity Press.)

8. Take the "Now or Later" portion of each study seriously. Consider how you need to apply the Scripture to your life. Remember that the group will follow your lead in responding to the studies. They will not go any deeper than you do.

Leading the Study

1. Begin the study on time. Open with prayer, asking God to help the group to understand and apply the passage.

2. Be sure that everyone in your group has a study guide. Encourage the group to prepare beforehand for each discussion by reading the introduction to the guide and by working through the questions in the study.

3. At the beginning of your first time together, explain that these studies are meant to be discussions, not lectures. Encourage the members of the group to participate. However, do not put pressure on those who may be hesitant to speak during the first few sessions.

4. Have a group member read the story in "Setting the Stage" at the beginning of the discussion or allow group members some time to read this silently. These stories are designed to draw the readers into the topic of the study and show how the topic is related to our daily lives. It is merely a starting point so don't allow the group members to get bogged down with details of the story or with trying to make a literal connection to the passage to be studied. Just enjoy them.

5. Every study begins with one or more "approach" questions, which are meant to be asked before the passage is read. These questions are designed to connect the opening story with the theme of the study and to encourage group members to begin to open up. Encourage as many members as possible to participate and be ready to get the discussion going with your own response.

Approach questions can reveal where our thoughts or feelings need to be transformed by Scripture. That is why it is especially important not to read the passage before the approach question is asked. The passage will tend to color the honest reactions people would otherwise give because they are, of course, supposed to think the way the Bible does.

6. Have a group member read aloud the passage to be studied.

7. As you ask the questions under "God's Word for Us," keep in mind that they are designed to be used just as they are written. You may simply read them aloud. Or you may prefer to express them in your own words.

There may be times when it is appropriate to deviate from the study guide. For example, a question may have already been answered. If so, move on to the next question. Or someone may raise an important question not covered in the guide. Take time to discuss it, but try to keep the group from going off on tangents.

8. Avoid answering your own questions. If necessary, repeat or rephrase them until they are clearly understood. An eager group quickly becomes passive and silent if they think the leader will do most of the talking.

9. Don't be afraid of silence. People may need time to think about the question before formulating their answers.

10. Don't be content with just one answer. Ask, "What do the rest of you think?" or "anything else?" until several people have given answers to the question.

11. Acknowledge all contributions. Try to be affirming whenever possible. Never reject an answer. If it is clearly off-base, ask, "Which verse led you to that conclusion?" or again, "What do the rest of you think?"

12. Don't expect every answer to be addressed to you, even though this will probably happen at first. As group members become more at ease, they will begin to truly interact with each other. This is one sign of healthy discussion.

13. Don't be afraid of controversy. It can be very stimulating. If you don't resolve an issue completely, don't be frustrated. Move on and keep it in mind for later. A subsequent study may solve the problem.

14. Periodically summarize what the group has said about the passage. This helps to draw together the various ideas mentioned and gives continuity to the study. But don't preach.

15. "Now or Later" can be used in a variety of ways depending on the time available to you and the interests of your group members. You may want to discuss an application question or idea and make some commitments. Or you may want to allow five minutes or so of quiet reflection within the group time so that people can journal their responses. Then, ask simply, "What did you experience (and/or learn) as you journaled?"

You will want to use at least one of these ideas to wrap up the group time, but you may want to encourage group members to continue working through other ideas throughout the week. You can continue discussing what has been learned at your next meeting.

16. Conclude your time together with conversational prayer. Ask for God in following through on the commitments you've made.

17. End on time.

Many more suggestions and helps are found in *Small Group Leaders' Handbook* and *The Big Book on Small Groups* (both from InterVarsity Press). Reading through one of these books would be worth your time.

Study Notes

General Note. You will see many references from the book *Keeping the Sabbath Wholly* by Marva J. Dawn (Eerdmans). It is an excellent book on the topic of rest and a great source for further reading.

Study 1. Jesus' Invitation to Rest. Matthew 11:28-30.
Purpose: To follow Christ's example and learn from him how to live life, which leads to the way of grace and rest for our souls.
Question 3. In order to receive Jesus' rest we need to recognize our need and then come to him. This is not a natural response on the part of human beings. The second condition is to make a choice to take his yoke upon yourself.
Question 5. If you are leading, think through this question before the meeting and be willing to share your needs honestly with the group. Don't rush past this question, and don't be afraid of silence as people ponder it. This is a question that is important to the study. If people don't look at what causes their weariness and burdens, it is difficult to know what to bring to Jesus.
Question 6. The rest Jesus offers is "Shalom" rest. This Hebrew term is a full bodied whole person rest which includes a sense of well-being and fulfillment, satisfaction, purpose, meaning in life, and peace with God the Father. It is a gift to be received. We cannot earn it.

Although physical rest is the first dimension that readily comes to mind when we think of rest, we can't begin immediately with that aspect because it is really impossible to rest our bodies thoroughly if our spirits are ill at ease.

We must discuss the dimension of spiritual resting first because we can truly learn how to rest only when we are genuinely freed by God's grace. . . . (Marva J. Dawn, *Keeping the Sabbath Wholly* [Grand Rapids, Mich.: Eerdmans, 1989], pp. 54-56.)

Spiritual rest leads to physical, emotional and psychological rest. After a tremendous victory showing up the pagan gods Elijah became depressed. First God gave him food and sleep. Then he dealt with Elijah's emotions. God met him in a new way—through a still, small voice. God loved him tenderly. He didn't criticize Elijah for his doubts and feelings but allowed him to express himself. He offers him time and space and gifts for emotional healing.

Question 7. In order to come to someone, you must leave where you are. Often when someone is called to faith in Christ they refuse because they don't want to leave the life they are living, they have become accustomed to particular sins or they want to run their own lives. They might be attracted to the person of Christ or even aware of their need for what he has to offer but do not want to leave where they are.

We who are followers of Jesus do not respond to his invitation to rest not because we don't want rest or believe that he can give it, but because we are not willing to move from where we are. Responding to his invitation might mean that working less at our profession or seeing less TV in order to be in his presence, or it might mean giving up bitterness toward another believer. It might mean I have to leave my comfort zone and be stretched a bit as I take on his yoke.

Question 8. As you think about what is attractive about learning from Jesus be clear as to what it means to learn from him. It is an act of submission. It is a statement of need—I need to learn something from him. The spiritual disciplines place us in a position to receive from God or to learn from him. It is good and fine for a student to ask questions.

Question 9. We learn to move through life as Jesus does, see things from his perspective and respond as he responds. There are two animals under a yoke. The older more experienced animal guides the younger less experienced one. In the same way Jesus shares the weight of our load and guides us through life. He demonstrates to us how to live.

With Jesus we find rest for our souls even in the midst of work. The work is easy and the burden is light. Our society sees rest as a reward for work. Jesus says that rest is a prerequisite for our work. We are not working alone, we are yoked to Jesus in relationship so that he carries most of the weight—a lifestyle of rest.

Study 2. God's Gift of Food and Rest. Exodus 16:1-30.

Purpose: To see how God provides what we need and encourages us to take time for regular Sabbath rest.

Question 2. Just three days have passed since the miracle of the Red Sea had occurred. The first twenty-one verses of chapter 15 are songs of praise and exaltation to God. Take time to look at the specific incidents as you consider the attitude of the Israelites. If you are leading you might ask, "What specific examples illustrate your answer?" This is a question intended to give an overview of the whole passage before coming back and looking at it more closely.

Question 4. If you are leading, allow time for reflection and encourage and model honesty.

Question 5. The reality is that God has placed us where we are and given us the people and circumstances in our lives. So when I rage about my neighbor or what I do or do not have, in reality I am raging against God who "brought me out of Egypt." Note that this question should not lead into a gossip session about people who may have offended us.

Question 7. When God's instructions were followed, we see that he faithfully met the needs of the Israelites in spite of their grumbling and lack of gratitude. He gave them careful instruction, told them what he would do for them and did all that he said he would do.

Question 8. In order for us to obey God and follow his instructions about regular rest we must believe in his faithfulness to us, that he will care for us, meet our needs and do what he says he will do.

> The spiritual rest which God especially intends in this commandment is not that we only cease from our labor and trade but much more—that we let God alone work in us and that in all our powers do we do nothing of our own. (Martin Luther)

Question 9. Often we blame the culture or say "I have to feed my family" when there are subtle needs and sinful motives that cause us to be driven. To the degree that the group is willing, look closely at the "attitudes of the heart."

Study 3. Resting in God's Power. Psalm 127.

Purpose: To learn how to work with a sense of confidence in God and to find peace from him in the midst of our work.

Question 2. Eugene Peterson gives the following commentary on Psalm 127:

> Work is a major component in most lives. It is unavoidable. It can be either good or bad, an area where our sin is magnified or where our faith matures. For it is the nature of sin to take good things and twist them, ever so slightly, so that they miss the target to which they were aimed, the target of God. . . .
>
> Psalm 127 shows both the right way and the wrong way to work. It posts a warning and provides the example which guide Christians in work that is done to the glory of God. (*A Long Obedience in the Same Direction* [Downers Grove, Ill.: InterVarsity Press, 1980], p. 101).

Question 4. This question is not meant to assume guilt. Not all Christians are moving about in "anxious toil." But many are. If you are in a group, you may find some who are living life with the sense that it is the Lord who is laboring, building and guarding. They should be free to voice this. Those who are struggling with a life full of anxiety must also have the freedom to share how their life is.

Question 5. Eugene Peterson responds to the idea that God is doing everything so we should sit back and do nothing.

> St. Paul had to deal with some of these people in the church at Thessalonica. They were saying that since God had done everything in Christ there was nothing more for them to do. If all effort ends up in godless confusion (as it did with the people at Babel) or in hypocritic self righteousness (as had happened among the Pharisees), the obvious and Christian solution is to quit work and wait for the Lord to come. . . .
>
> Meanwhile they lived "by faith" off their less spiritual friends. Unfriendly critics might have called them freeloaders. Paul became angry and told them to get to work: "We hear that some of you are living in idleness, mere busybodies, not doing any work. Now such persons we command and exhort in the Lord Jesus Christ to do their work in quietness and to earn their own living. Brethren, do not be weary in well-doing" (2 Thess. 3:11-13). . . .
>
> Psalm 127 shows a way to work which is neither sheer activity nor pure passivity. It doesn't glorify work as such and it doesn't say, "God has a great work for you to do; go and do it." Nor does it say, "God has done everything; go fishing." If we want simple

solutions in regard to work we can become workaholics or drop-outs. If we want to experience the fullness of work, we will do better to study Psalm 127. (*Obedience*, pp. 102-3)

Question 6. It is a distinctive of Christians that we take God seriously. We believe that he is the central reality of all existence. We pay attention to what he is and to what he does. We live in response to that reality and not to some other. Paying attention to God involves a realization that he works.

Before anything else, work is an activity of God. . . . The curse of some people's lives is not work, as such, but senseless work, vain work, futile work, work that takes place apart from God. . . . Work has dignity: there can be nothing degrading about work if God works. Work has purpose: there can be nothing futile about work if God works. (Peterson, *Obedience*, pp. 104-5.)

Question 7. Peterson points out "In contrast to the anxious labor that builds cities and guards possessions, the psalm praises the effortless work of making children." In birthing children we are participants who look on in wonder at God's miraculous creation (*Obedience*, Peterson, p. 104).

It is difficult to study this passage without asking the question, "How often are children perceived today as a heritage? For those who are infertile to say that the work of making children is "effort-less" is too simplistic. In fact, this portion of Scripture may be a great source of pain. If you are leading a group, you may find that they would like to talk about their pain.

One such woman said to me, "I have 'toiled in vain' for years to have a child. I found this study still to be applicable. God's rest and peace came only when I stopped 'toiling' and accepted his will and direction."

The goal is not to give answers or even to say "stop toiling" to group members, but to lovingly listen and care for and pray for anyone you find in this kind of pain.

Question 8. There are many ways that building a house is like building a family. Think about what children bring to our lives. It seems like they might even bring an element of protection (v. 5).

As in the first portion of this passage, we don't just sit back and do nothing because "the Lord builds the house," so with rearing our children, we don't just sit back and assume God will do everything. Yet we cannot do it all alone: "unless the Lord builds the house, the labor is in vain." We listen to his voice, give input into our kids lives according to his instructions through his Word, pray, love and have confidence only because the Lord does the work.

Study 4. Resting in God's Presence. Exodus 33:1-17.

Purpose: To see from Moses' life that there is no greater sense of rest than to live moment by moment in God's presence, knowing that what we do matters to him.

Question 3. Look at this section closely. Consider what God must have felt. Enter into Moses' frustration and the distress of the Israelites. Verses 3-6 seem to describe a people who are experiencing the opposite of rest. When people are in mourning, it is impossible to sleep. There probably were tears and distress.

The people were told to take off their ornaments. This was a further statement of God's disapproval of their actions. They had received these ornaments at the time they left Egypt. According to the *New Bible Commentary*, "Their removal like the discarding of an engagement ring, symbolized the broken relationship which now existed between God and the people" (21st Century Edition [Downers Grove, Ill.: InterVarsity Press, 1994], p. 117). The people feared for their lives.

Question 4. For a better understanding of the "Tent of Meeting" see Exodus 29:42-44 and 40:34.

> Verses 42-43 [in Exodus 29] highlight the purpose of these instructions: the establishment of the sacrificial ritual was a necessary requirement before God could meet with the Israelites. As God affirmed "there I will meet with the Israelites, and the place will be consecrated by my glory"(43). As v 46 makes clear, the ultimate purpose of God's deliverance of the Israelites from Egypt was so that he might dwell among them. (*New Bible Commentary*, p. 115.)

Question 5. It may be helpful to add some information on the meaning of "tent of meeting." According to Marva Dawn, in Jewish Sabbath prayers God is asked to embrace his people "with the tent of his peace." She explains the symbolism of the tent "connotes the presence of God in a very special way. When the earliest people of Israel wandered in the wilderness, their tent of God's presence was particularly visited with Yahweh's glory" (*Sabbath*, pp. 63-64).

Question 6. By this time the Israelites had spent almost forty years in the wilderness disobeying and rebelling against God. God promised to send them an angel and said their enemies would be driven out of the land—despite their repeated sin. Yet when God spoke of sending them off without his presence, they were in distress. Consider how you ignore God's warnings and continue in sin and yet question God when you face consequences.

Question 7. Look at this portion of the passage carefully and allow time to respond thoroughly. The conversation between God and Moses is powerful. Moses reminds God of what he was called to do and what God has promised. Moses longs to know God even more deeply and to find more favor with him. He asks God to teach him his ways so that this can happen. Even in the midst of this somewhat scary and frustrating situation, Moses refuses to go up from that place if God does not go with him.

Question 10. Define rest based on the words of God, "My Presence will go with you, and I will give you rest" (v. 14). You have already looked at what happened to the Israelites when God threatened to withdraw his presence. Look also at how Moses was affected when God promised his presence.

Rest in this passage means a "sense of well being"—spiritually, emotionally, physically. It means safety, peace, quietness. It seems to mean that when my relationship with God is intact, I am communicating openly with him, I have his approval, I am not in rebellion—that all is well no matter what I have yet to face. According to Marva Dawn, "The greatest result of Sabbath resting is the opportunity to know the presence of God, no matter what our present circumstances might be" (*Sabbath*, p. 61).

Study 5. Resting in Belief in God. Hebrews 3:1—4:11.
Purpose: To look at the different dimensions of God's rest and to understand that entering this rest involves choice, belief and obedience on our part.

General Note. Hebrews is written to Jewish Christians who had not "fully broken with Judaism or fully embraced Christianity" to help them understand the distinctives of Christianity. (Thomas Hewitt, *The Epistle to the Hebrews* [Grand Rapids: Eerdmans, 1979], p. 40.)

Question 2. This is a difficult, but important, passage. Not all the ideas about God's rest and what each reference to rest means is clear. Some in your group may disagree on the interpretation. Give freedom for this. And do not get bogged down and miss the richness of the passage. This question is meant to help give an overview of the passage. The point is to see that there are many dimensions to God's rest. Many of the aspects of God's rest in these studies can be seen in this passage. Some of the references to "rest" have more than one meaning or dimension.

The "rest" in 3:11 refers to the Promised Land that was promised to the Israelites after God led them out of Egypt. Verses 7-11 of this passage are quoted from Psalm 95:7-11.

The "rest" in 3:18 refers to the same Promised Land as 3:11 into which this generation of Israelites was not allowed to enter because of their unbelief.

The "rest" in 4:1 is spoken of in present tense and is a standing invitation of God. It is the rest of a relationship with himself.

The "rest" in 4:3 can still be entered. The writer states that those who believe enter that rest. The "rest" in the second part of 4:3 is in the past tense and refers back to God's refusing to allow the Israelites to enter the Promised Land (see Hebrews 3:11 and Psalm 95:11).

In 4:4 the "rest" refers to God's ceasing from his labor on the seventh day after working six days to create the world.

In 4:6 the "rest" refers to both the past rest of the Promised Land and to the present rest—a relationship with God.

In 4:8 Joshua's "rest" is the rest of entering the Promised Land. That rest was not enough and God speaks of another day of "rest."

In 4:9-11 the Sabbath rest refers to eternal rest in heaven. We rest from our labor just as God rested from the physical work of creation.

If you are leading a group, don't think that you have to give your group all this information. This note is meant to help you have the different rests straight in your mind so that you can give extra information as needed. It is also meant to help you be ready for the next question.

Question 3. This is a second overview question to focus on the varied references to the Old Testament and the connections between the many kinds of rest dealt with in this passage. Keep in mind that the nation of Israel had been miraculously led out of Egypt by Moses: the Red Sea parted for them to go through and then came back together and drown the Egyptians who were on their trail. Instead of going into the Promised Land that God had already prepared for them, they refused. They were afraid, in spite of what God told them, that they would be defeated by the occupants of the land. They ended up wandering in the wilderness for forty years.

As with the Israelites, through grace, the way of rest is open to those who believe. But we also can fail to enter because of unbelief. Rejection of grace produces hardness of heart.

Question 4. Identifying and recognizing the place of Moses was important. It was even more important to recognize Jesus' superiority. Look closely at who Jesus is as stated in verses 1-6. According to the *New Bible Commentary:*

> The focus is first on the faithfulness of Jesus as 'the apostle and high priest whom we confess.' This is developed by contrasting Jesus with Moses who was the key figure in the establishment of Israel as God's 'house' (household or family) at the time of the exodus. The writer's argument would have had special point for Jewish Christians tempted to drift back into Judaism, where Moses and the revelation he brought to Israel were held in such high regard. But the passage has broader application because of the positive things that are said about Jesus. (p. 1328)

Question 6. Sin is "almost personified" in these verses. "It deceives the sinner, exaggerating the satisfaction that can be gained from sin, then blinds his mind to spiritual truth and also the certainty of God's retribution. It is possible that sin had already deceived some of the readers by giving them a romantic faithfulness to the past and by blinding them to the dangers so clearly brought out in this Epistle" (*Hebrews*, p. 84).

If you are leading a group, and it feels appropriate, have them discuss how they have been deceived by sin.

Question 7. Just because the Israelites did not believe God and perished rather than enter the rest of the Promised Land, it did not negate the promise that some would enter God's rest. Neither was the promise of rest completely fulfilled when the next generation of Israelites entered the promised land. The Promised Land of Canaan was only a type of God's rest. The promise to enter God's rest still stands. The writer suggests that they examine themselves so that they don't make the same mistake that those who did not enter the

Promised Land made. In order for this message or invitation to be of value to them it must be accepted or combined with faith. Those who believe God enter his rest, a relationship of forgiveness with himself.

Question 10. According to the *New Bible Commentary:*

The rest that the Israelites experienced in the time of Joshua was an earthly anticipation of the ultimate, heavenly rest. Hebrews goes on to argue that the way into that ultimate inheritance has been secured by the Lord Jesus Christ. A long time after the conquest of Canaan, Ps 95 designated another day as the day (Today) to hear his voice and enter God's rest. this proves that David had in mind a rest beyond the enjoyment of life in the land of Israel. If Joshua had given his people ultimate rest at the time of the conquest, God would not have spoken later of another day. The hope of God's people is a heavenly rest, not the reestablishing of the Jews in the land of Israel. The fundamental promises of the old covenant are fulfilled in a transformed way by Christ. (p. 1331)

Question 13. This is a review question to help the group look at all the dimensions of rest that are covered in this passage. There is rest from physical labor, there is spiritual rest which comes from a right relationship with God, and there is the rest of Heaven—eternal rest where we will never have to work at anything again.

Study 6. Resting in God's Purpose. Luke 2:21-40.

Purpose: To understand that God has a purpose for each of us and what it means to wait in hope and to experience the rest which that attitude brings to life.

Question 4. We will be looking at Simeon and Anna throughout this study and comparing their lives of rest and hope as they waited for God's purpose to be fulfilled in "the fullness of time." Look closely at who they are and how they walked with the Lord.

Question 5. The promise and word of the Lord had great power in Simeon's life. He believed God and waited.

Anna was a prophetess. This title suggests that she too had been told ahead of time what God was going to do and that Jesus was coming. It seems too like there was a circular affect. God revealed to Anna his purpose and that led to prayer and worship and in the midst of prayer and worship is how we see and hear God more clearly.

Question 7. Do not pass over this question quickly. Take time to evaluate your view of God and how your conviction about his purposes affects you.

Question 13. If you are leading a group, at the end of this study you might ask a review question about the whole guide such as "What difference has studying these passages made in your ability and desire to rest?" or "What have you learned throughout this study guide concerning rest?" or "What specific ways do you want to apply what you have learned?"

Other InterVarsity Press Bible Studies by Phyllis J. Le Peau

LifeGuide® Bible Studies
Acts
Ephesians (with Andrew T. Le Peau)
James (with Andrew T. Le Peau)
Love
Women of the New Testament

Caring People Bible Studies
Handbook for Caring People (with Bonnie J. Miller)
Resources for Caring People
The Character of Caring People
Caring for Spiritual Needs
Caring for Emotional Needs
Caring for Physical Needs
Caring for People in Grief

Novels by Linda Shands
Seasons Remembered Series
A Time to Keep
A Time to Embrace
A Time to Search
A Time to Speak

All books and Bible studies are from InterVarsity Press and are available at your local Christian bookstore. Visit our web site at www.ivpress.com for more information and for "The Small Group Doctor" column. E-mail us with your feedback on this guide at doctor@ivpress.com.